The MAILBOX®
The Education Center®

Phenomenal Phonics®

grades

W9-BNA-821

Phonics Games

Reproducible Lotto Games for Reinforcing

- **Lowercase and uppercase letters**
- **Beginning sounds**
- **Digraphs**

Managing Editor: Gerri Primak

Editorial Team: Becky S. Andrews, Kimberley Bruck, Karen P. Shelton, Diane Badden, Thad H. McLaurin, Sharon Murphy, Lynn Drolet, Kelly Robertson, Karen A. Brudnak, Juli Docimo Blair, Hope Rodgers, Dorothy C. McKinney

Production Team: Lori Z. Henry, Pam Crane, Rebecca Saunders, Jennifer Tipton Cappoen, Chris Curry, Sarah Foreman, Theresa Lewis Goode, Greg D. Rieves, Eliseo De Jesus Santos II, Barry Slate, Donna K. Teal, Zane Williard, Tazmen Carlisle, Marsha Heim, Lynette Dickerson, Mark Rainey, Karen Brewer Grossman

Reproducible
Assessments
Also
Included!

www.themailbox.com

©2007 The Mailbox®
All rights reserved.
ISBN10 #1-56234-747-0 • ISBN13 #978-156234-747-5

Manufactured in the United States
10 9 8 7 6 5 4 3 2 1

Table of Contents

Lotto Games

Assessments

What's Inside

Phonics Games contains ten reproducible lotto games, each reinforcing a different skill. Each game includes the following:

- directions for the teacher
- six different reproducible gameboards
- reproducible teacher cards
- a reproducible follow-up assessment page

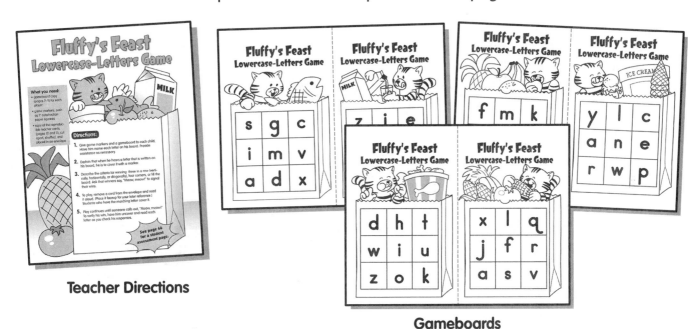

Teacher Directions

Gameboards

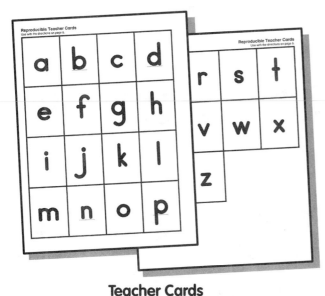

Teacher Cards

Assessment Page

Also Included:

- assessment pages to review beginning sounds and beginning letters
- reproducible student brag tags
- reproducible storage labels

Brag Tags

Copy on colorful construction paper, cut out, and use as rewards for each game.

Fluffy's Feast
Lowercase-Letters Game

What you need:
- gameboard copy (pages 7–9) for each player
- game markers, such as 1" construction paper squares
- copy of the reproducible teacher cards (pages 10 and 11), cut apart, shuffled, and placed in an envelope

Directions:

1. Give game markers and a gameboard to each child. Have him name each letter on his board. Provide assistance as necessary.

2. Explain that when he hears a letter that is written on his board, he is to cover it with a marker.

3. Describe the criteria for winning: three in a row (vertically, horizontally, or diagonally), four corners, or fill the board. Ask that winners say, "Meow, meow!" to signal their wins.

4. To play, remove a card from the envelope and read it aloud. (Place it faceup for your later reference.) Students who have the matching letter cover it.

5. Play continues until someone calls out, "Meow, meow!" To verify his win, have him uncover and read each letter as you check his responses.

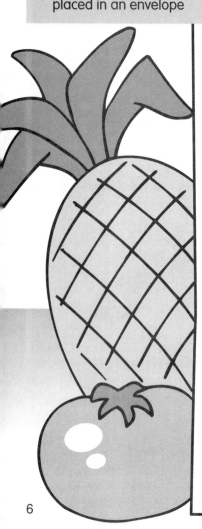

See page 66 for a student assessment page.

Fluffy's Feast
Lowercase-Letters Game

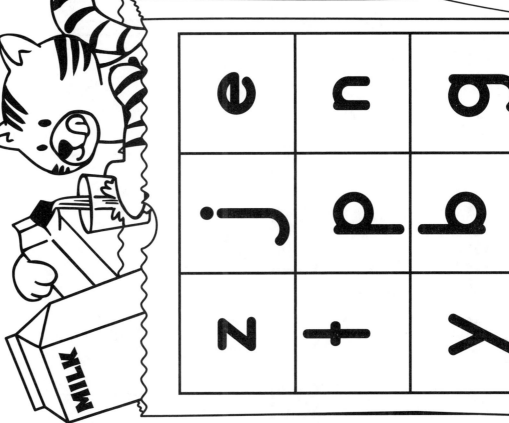

e	j	z
n	p	t
g	b	y

©The Mailbox® • Phenomenal Phonics® Games • TEC61061

Fluffy's Feast
Lowercase-Letters Game

c	g	s
v	m	i
x	p	a

©The Mailbox® • Phenomenal Phonics® Games • TEC61061

7

Fluffy's Feast
Lowercase-Letters Game

y	l	c
a	n	e
r	w	p

Fluffy's Feast
Lowercase-Letters Game

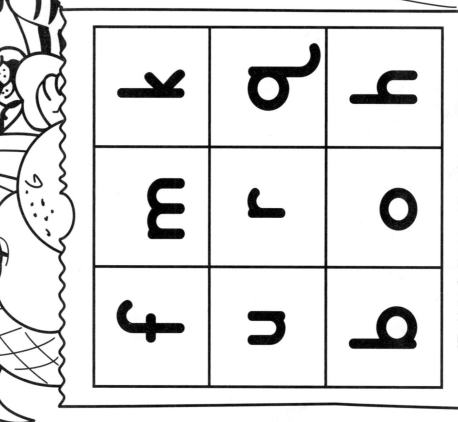

f	m	k
u	r	q
b	o	h

8

Fluffy's Feast
Lowercase-Letters Game

l	x
q	

f	j
r	J

s	a
v	

Fluffy's Feast
Lowercase-Letters Game

h	p
t	

i	w
u	

o	z
k	

a	b	c	d
TEC61061	TEC61061	TEC61061	TEC61061
e	f	g	h
TEC61061	TEC61061	TEC61061	TEC61061
i	j	k	l
TEC61061	TEC61061	TEC61061	TEC61061
m	n	o	p
TEC61061	TEC61061	TEC61061	TEC61061

©The Mailbox® • *Phenomenal Phonics® Games* • TEC61061

q	r	s	t
TEC61061	TEC61061	TEC61061	TEC61061
u	v	w	x
TEC61061	TEC61061	TEC61061	TEC61061
y	z		
TEC61061	TEC61061		

Up, Up, and Away!
Uppercase-Letters Game

What you need:
- gameboard copy (pages 13–15) for each player
- game markers, such as 1" construction paper squares
- copy of the reproducible teacher cards (pages 16 and 17), cut apart, shuffled, and placed in an envelope

Directions:

1. Give game markers and a gameboard to each child. Have her name each letter on her board. Provide assistance as necessary.

2. Explain that when she hears a letter that is written on her board, she is to cover it with a marker.

3. Describe the criteria for winning: three in a row (vertically, horizontally, or diagonally), four corners, or fill the board. Ask that winners say, "Up, up, and away!" to signal their wins.

4. To play, remove a card from the envelope and read it aloud. (Place it faceup for your later reference.) Students who have the matching letter cover it.

5. Play continues until someone calls out, "Up, up, and away!" To verify her win, have her uncover and read each letter as you check her responses.

See page 67 for a student assessment page.

Up, Up, and Away!
Uppercase-Letters Game

N	Y	S
X	U	H
J	P	B

Up, Up, and Away!
Uppercase-Letters Game

H	V	A
R	D	N
L	Z	F

Up, Up, and Away!
Uppercase-Letters Game

D	W	G
K	B	I
P	M	R

Up, Up, and Away!
Uppercase-Letters Game

C	E	O
Q	W	A
I	L	U

14

Up, Up, and Away!
Uppercase-Letters Game

Y	J	M
F	S	D
Q	C	T

Up, Up, and Away!
Uppercase-Letters Game

V	S	T
K	E	G
Z	O	J

A TEC61061	B TEC61061	C TEC61061	D TEC61061
E TEC61061	F TEC61061	G TEC61061	H TEC61061
I TEC61061	J TEC61061	K TEC61061	L TEC61061
M TEC61061	N TEC61061	O TEC61061	P TEC61061

Q	R	S	T
TEC61061	TEC61061	TEC61061	TEC61061
U	V	W	X
TEC61061	TEC61061	TEC61061	TEC61061
Y	Z		
TEC61061	TEC61061		

Out of This World
Uppercase- and Lowercase- Letters Game

What you need:
- gameboard copy (pages 19–21) for each player
- game markers, such as 1" construction paper squares
- copy of the reproducible teacher cards (pages 22 and 23), cut apart, shuffled, and placed in an envelope

Directions:

1. Give game markers and a gameboard to each child. Have him name each letter on his board. Provide assistance as necessary.

2. Explain that when he hears a letter that is written on his board, he is to cover it with a marker.

3. Describe the criteria for winning: five in a row horizontally, four corners, or fill the board. Ask that winners say, "Zoom! Zoom!" to signal their wins.

4. To play, remove a card from the envelope, announce whether the letter is uppercase or lowercase, and read it aloud. (Place it faceup for your later reference.) Students who have the matching letter cover it.

5. Play continues until someone calls out, "Zoom! Zoom!" To verify his win, have him uncover and read the uppercase and the lowercase letters as you check his responses.

See page 68 for a student assessment page.

Out of This World
Uppercase- and Lowercase-Letters Game

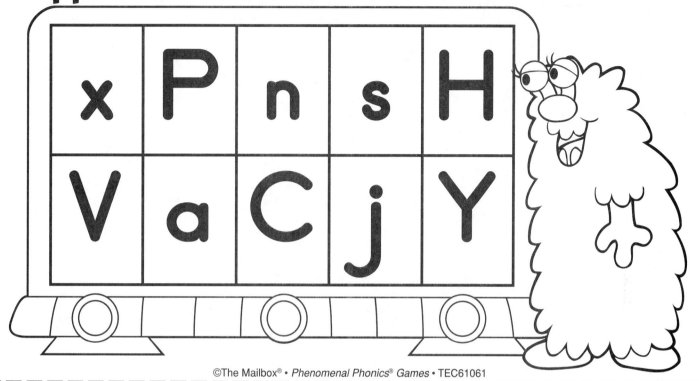

x	P	n	s	H
V	a	C	j	Y

Out of This World
Uppercase- and Lowercase-Letters Game

L	r	T	B	g
c	W	E	z	p

Out of This World
Uppercase- and Lowercase-Letters Game

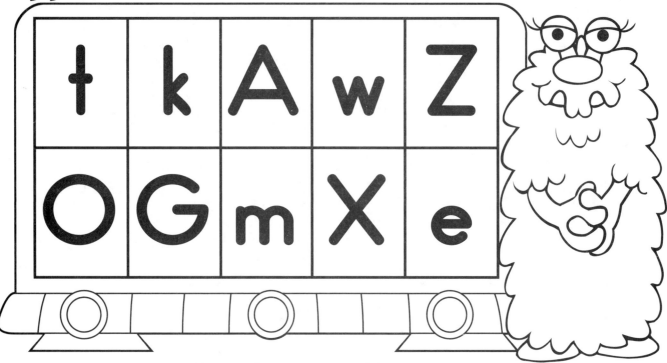

t	k	A	w	Z
O	G	m	X	e

Out of This World
Uppercase- and Lowercase-Letters Game

N	u	Q	i	K
d	Y	l	F	r

Out of This World
Uppercase- and Lowercase-Letters Game

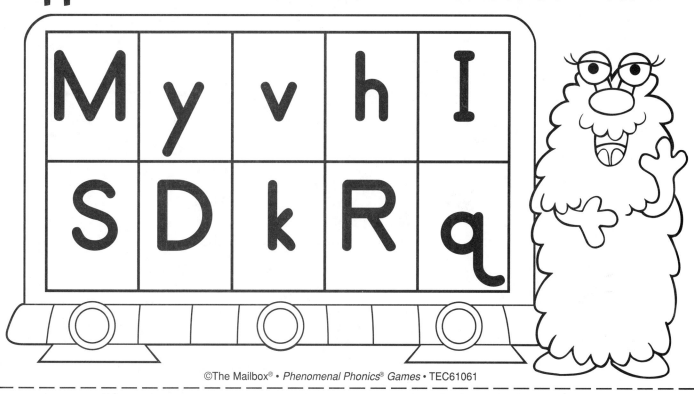

M	y	v	h	I
S	D	k	R	q

Out of This World
Uppercase- and Lowercase-Letters Game

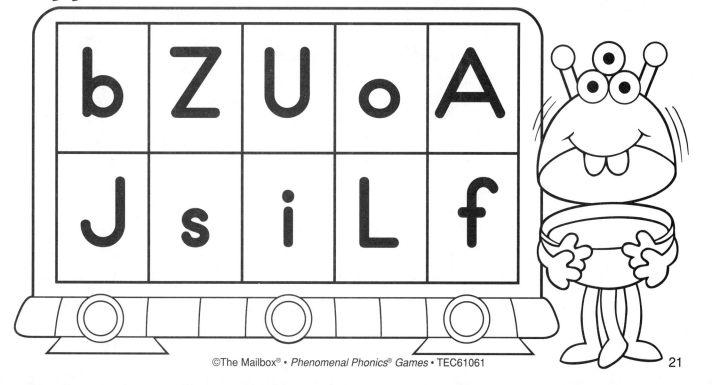

b	Z	U	o	A
J	s	i	L	f

Reproducible Teacher Cards
Use with the directions on page 18.

A TEC61061				
B TEC61061	**C** TEC61061	**D** TEC61061	**E** TEC61061	**F** TEC61061
G TEC61061	**H** TEC61061	**I** TEC61061	**J** TEC61061	**K** TEC61061
L TEC61061	**M** TEC61061	**N** TEC61061	**O** TEC61061	**P** TEC61061
Q TEC61061	**R** TEC61061	**S** TEC61061	**T** TEC61061	**U** TEC61061
V TEC61061	**W** TEC61061	**X** TEC61061	**Y** TEC61061	**Z** TEC61061

©The Mailbox® • *Phenomenal Phonics® Games* • TEC61061

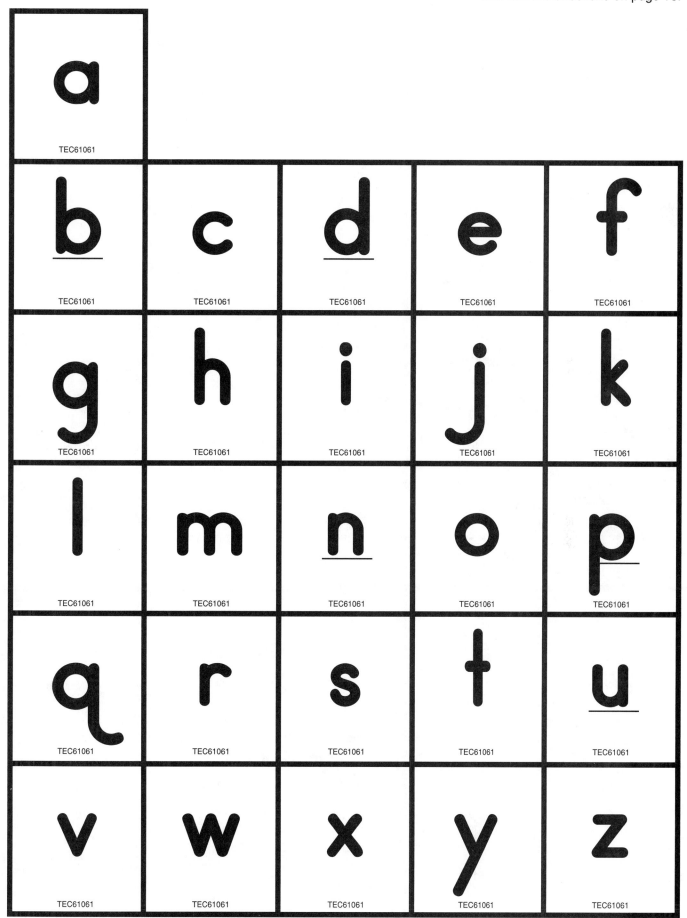

a				
TEC61061				

b	c	d	e	f
TEC61061	TEC61061	TEC61061	TEC61061	TEC61061

g	h	i	j	k
TEC61061	TEC61061	TEC61061	TEC61061	TEC61061

l	m	n	o	p
TEC61061	TEC61061	TEC61061	TEC61061	TEC61061

q	r	s	t	u
TEC61061	TEC61061	TEC61061	TEC61061	TEC61061

v	w	x	y	z
TEC61061	TEC61061	TEC61061	TEC61061	TEC61061

School Tools
Beginning-Sounds Game
/f/, /m/, /r/, /s/, /t/

What you need:
- gameboard copy (pages 25–27) for each player
- game markers, such as 1" construction paper squares
- copy of the reproducible teacher cards (pages 28 and 29), cut apart, shuffled, and placed in an envelope

Directions:

1. Give game markers and a gameboard to each child. Have her name each picture on her board. Provide assistance as necessary.

2. Explain that when she hears a word, she listens for its beginning sound. If she has a picture on her board whose name starts with the same beginning sound, she is to cover it with a marker.

3. Describe the criteria for winning: three in a row (vertically, horizontally, or diagonally) or four corners. Ask that winners say, "School is cool!" to signal their wins.

4. To play, remove a card from the envelope and name the picture. If desired, also show students the picture card. (Place it faceup for your later reference.) Students who have a picture with the same beginning sound cover it. (A child may cover only one picture at a time.)

5. Play continues until someone calls out, "School is cool!" To verify her win, have her uncover and say the name of each picture and its beginning sound as you check her responses.

See page 69 for a student assessment page.

24

School Tools
Beginning-Sounds Game

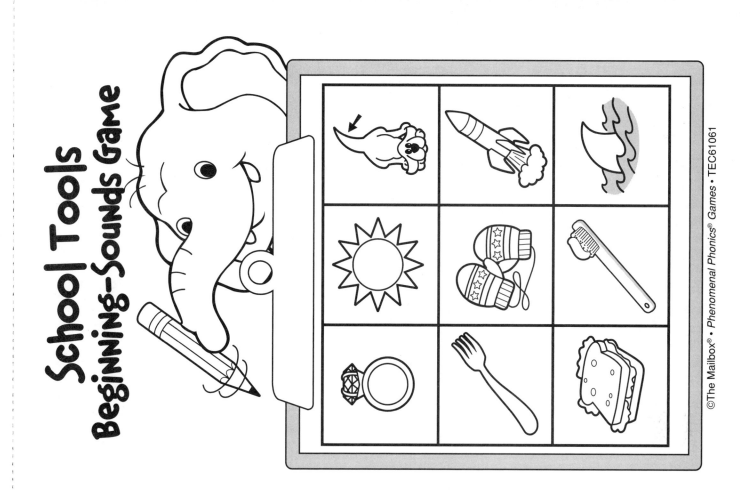

School Tools
Beginning-Sounds Game

School Tools
Beginning-Sounds Game

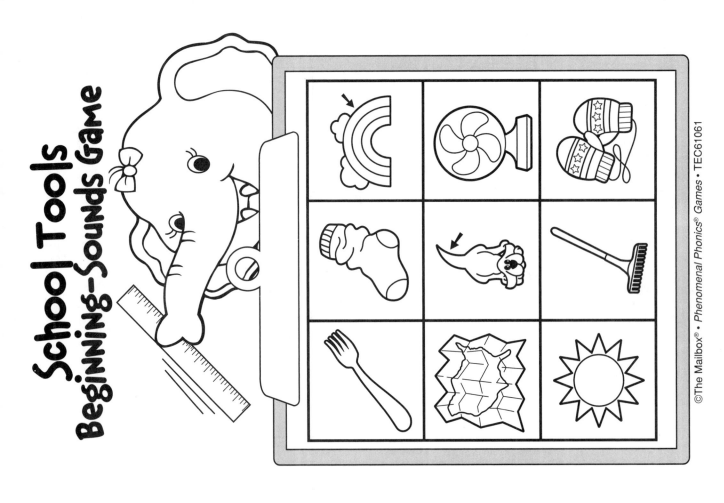

School Tools
Beginning-Sounds Game

School Tools
Beginning-Sounds Game

School Tools
Beginning-Sounds Game

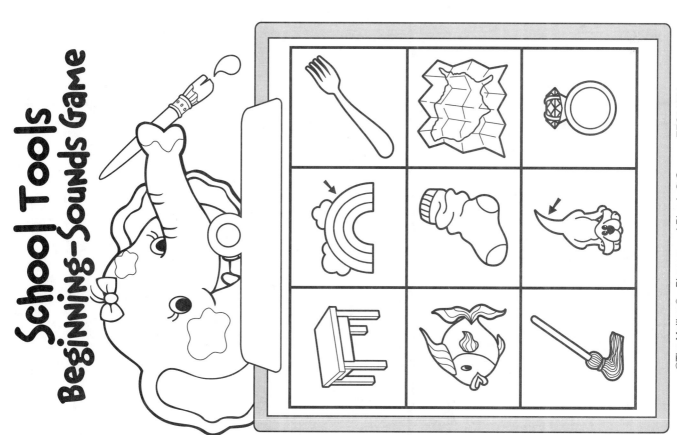

Reproducible Teacher Cards

Use with the directions on page 24.

TEC61061

TEC61061

TEC61061

TEC61061

TEC61061

TEC61061

TEC61061

TEC61061

TEC61061

TEC61061

Bookworm's Notes
Beginning-Sounds Game

/d/, /k/, /n/, /p/, /w/

What you need:

- gameboard copy (pages 31–33) for each player

- game markers, such as 1" construction paper squares

- copy of the reproducible teacher cards (pages 34 and 35), cut apart, shuffled, and placed in an envelope

Directions:

1. Give game markers and a gameboard to each child. Have him name each picture on his board. Provide assistance as necessary.

2. Explain that when he hears a word, he listens for its beginning sound. If he has a picture on his board whose name starts with the same beginning sound, he is to cover it with a marker.

3. Describe the criteria for winning: three in a row (vertically, horizontally, or diagonally) or four corners. Ask that winners say, "Bookworm!" to signal their wins.

4. To play, remove a card from the envelope and name the picture. If desired, also show students the picture card. (Place it faceup for your later reference.) Students who have a picture with the same beginning sound cover it. (A child may cover only one picture at a time.)

5. Play continues until someone calls out "Bookworm!" To verify his win, have him uncover and say the name of each picture and its beginning sound as you check his responses.

See page 70 for a student assessment page.

Bookworm's Notes
Beginning-Sounds Game

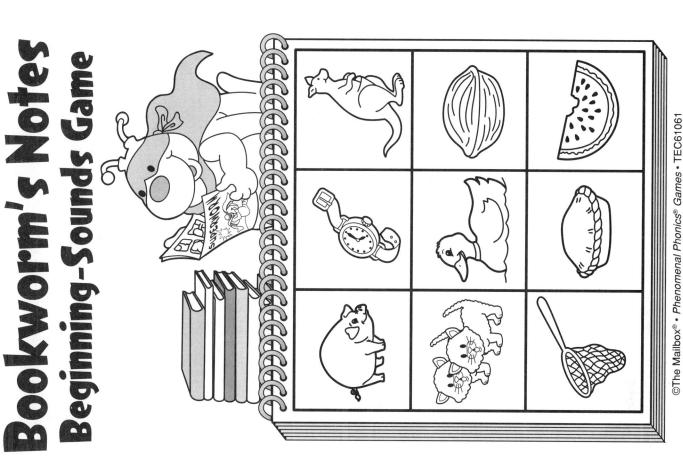

Bookworm's Notes
Beginning-Sounds Game

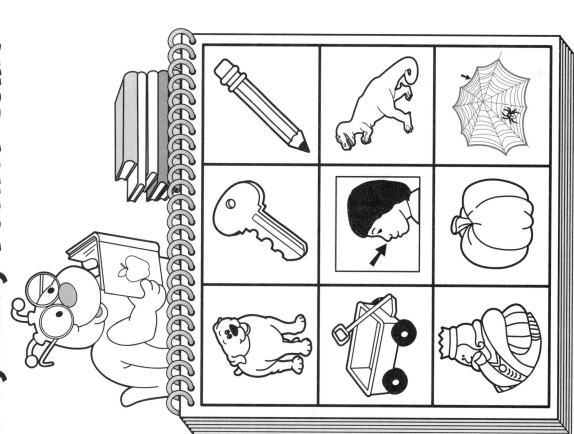

Bookworm's Notes
Beginning-Sounds Game

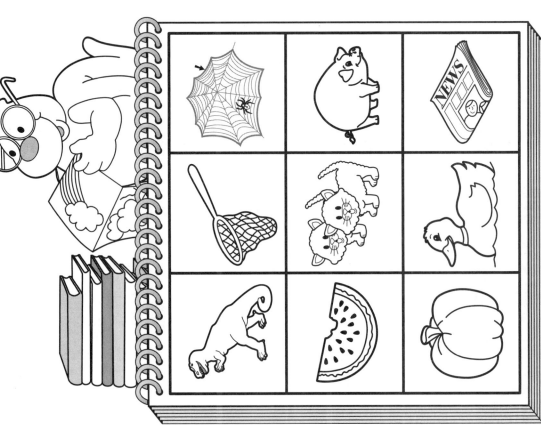

Bookworm's Notes
Beginning-Sounds Game

Bookworm's Notes
Beginning-Sounds Game

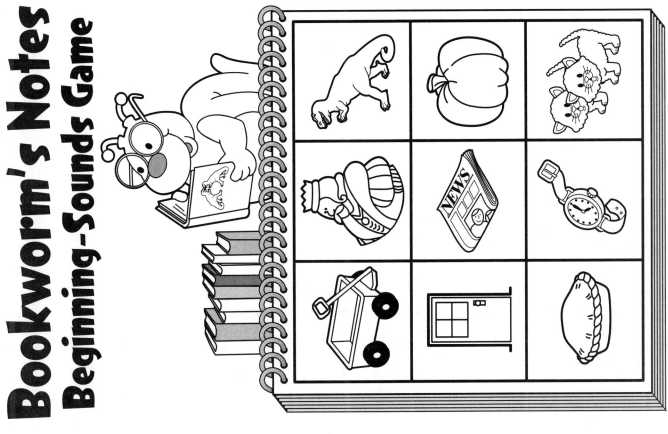

Bookworm's Notes
Beginning-Sounds Game

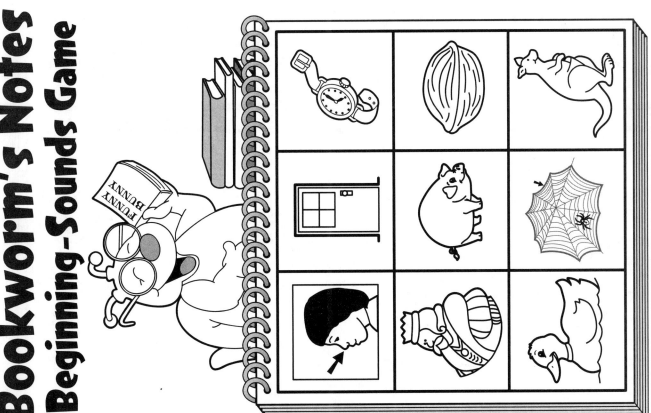

Reproducible Teacher Cards
Use with the directions on page 30.

TEC61061

TEC61061

TEC61061

TEC61061

TEC61061

TEC61061

TEC61061

TEC61061

TEC61061

TEC61061

Dragon Friends Beginning-Sounds Game

/b/, /g/, /h/, /v/, /z/

What you need:

- gameboard copy (pages 37–39) for each player
- game markers, such as 1" construction paper squares
- copy of the reproducible teacher cards (pages 40 and 41), cut apart, shuffled, and placed in an envelope

Directions:

1. Give game markers and a gameboard to each child. Have her name each picture on her board. Provide assistance as necessary.

2. Explain that when she hears a word, she listens for its beginning sound. If she has a picture on her board whose name starts with the same beginning sound, she is to cover it with a marker.

3. Describe the criteria for winning: three in a row (vertically, horizontally, or diagonally) or four corners. Ask that winners say, "Dragon friends!" to signal their wins.

4. To play, remove a card from the envelope and name the picture. If desired, also show students the picture card. (Place it faceup for your later reference.) Students who have a picture with the same beginning sound cover it. (A child may cover only one picture at a time.)

5. Play continues until someone calls out, "Dragon friends!" To verify her win, have her uncover and say the name of each picture and its beginning sound as you check her responses.

See page 71 for a student assessment page.

Dragon Friends
Beginning-Sounds Game

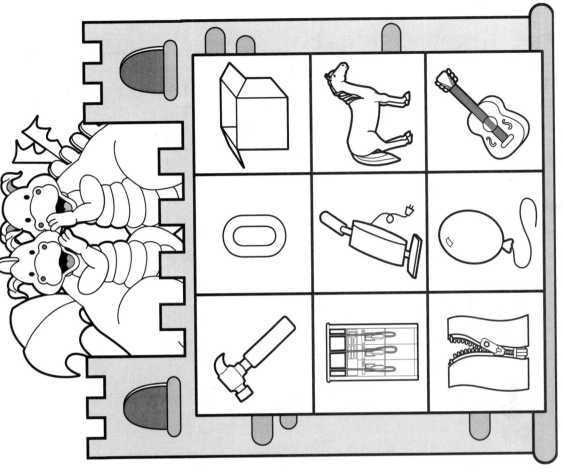

Dragon Friends
Beginning-Sounds Game

Dragon Friends
Beginning-Sounds Game

Dragon Friends
Beginning-Sounds Game

Dragon Friends
Beginning-Sounds Game

Dragon Friends
Beginning-Sounds Game

Reproducible Teacher Cards

Use with the directions on page 36.

TEC61061

TEC61061

TEC61061

TEC61061

TEC61061

TEC61061

TEC61061

TEC61061

TEC61061

TEC61061

Look Who's Reading
Beginning-Letters Game
j, n, r, s, t

What you need:
- gameboard copy (pages 43–45) for each player
- game markers, such as 1" construction paper squares
- copy of the reproducible teacher cards (pages 46 and 47), cut apart, shuffled, and placed in an envelope

Directions:

1. Give game markers and a gameboard to each child. Have him name each picture on his board. Provide assistance as necessary.

2. Explain that when he hears a letter that is the beginning letter of a picture on his board, he is to cover the picture with a marker.

3. Describe the criteria for winning: three in a row (vertically, horizontally, or diagonally) or four corners. Ask that winners say, "Hoot! Hoot!" to signal their wins.

4. To play, remove a card from the envelope and read the letter aloud. (Place it faceup for later reference.) Students who have a picture that begins with the named letter cover it. (A child may cover only one picture at a time.)

5. Play continues until someone calls out, "Hoot! Hoot!" To verify his win, have the child uncover and say the name of each picture and its beginning letter as you check his responses.

See page 73 for a student assessment page.

Look Who's Reading
Beginning-Letters Game

Look Who's Reading
Beginning-Letters Game

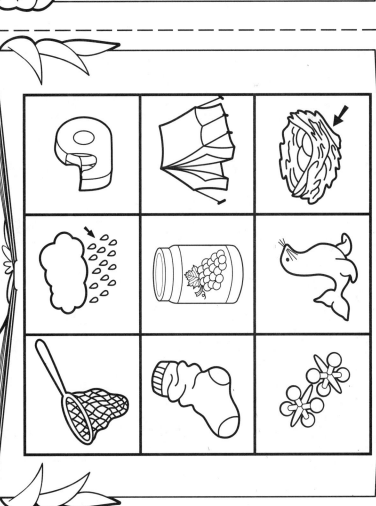

Look Who's Reading
Beginning-Letters Game

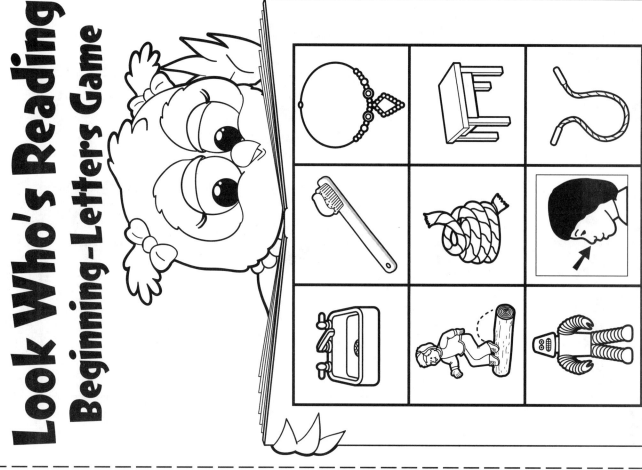

Look Who's Reading
Beginning-Letters Game

44

Look Who's Reading
Beginning-Letters Game

Look Who's Reading
Beginning-Letters Game

Reproducible Teacher Cards

Use with the directions on page 42.

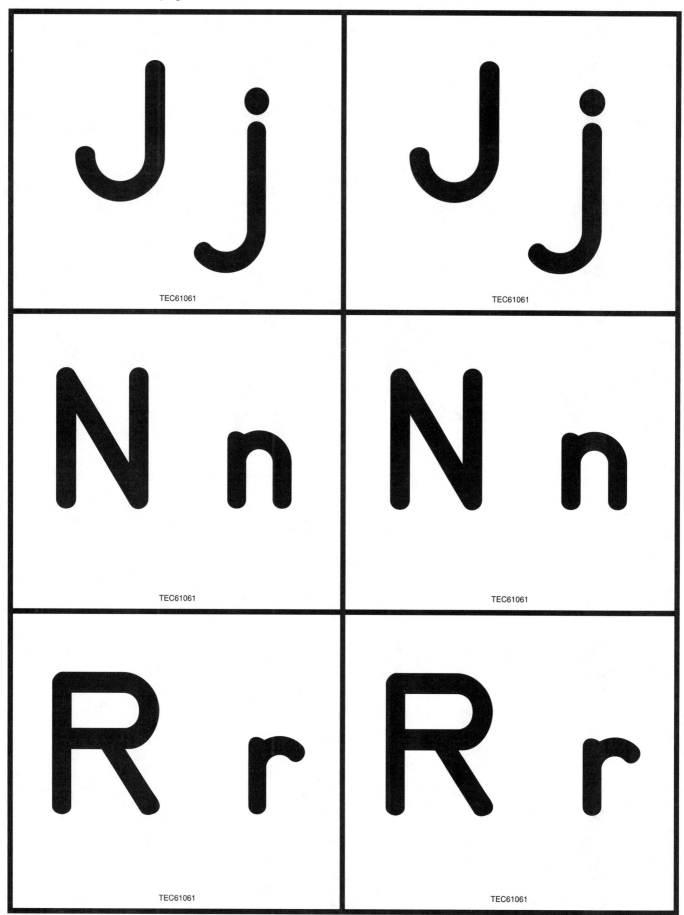

J j   TEC61061

J j   TEC61061

N n   TEC61061

N n   TEC61061

R r   TEC61061

R r   TEC61061

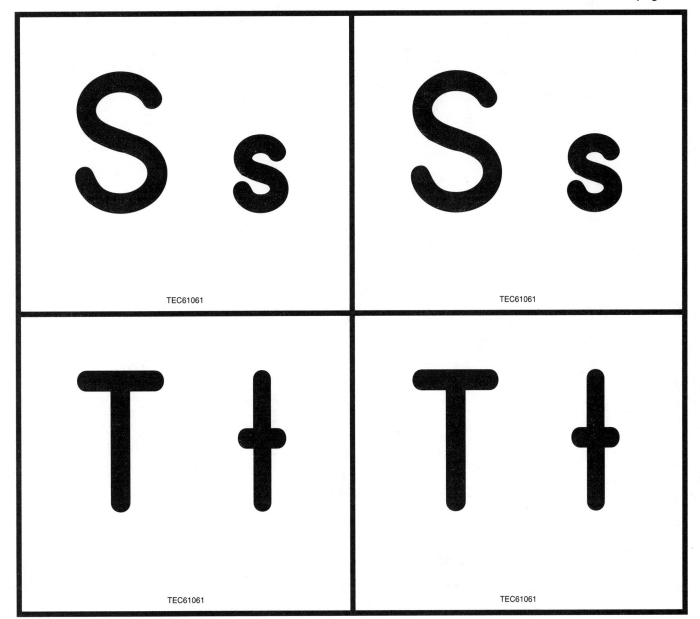

Sweet Dreams
Beginning-Letters Game
b, c, h, m, w

See page 74 for a student assessment page.

What you need:
- gameboard copy (pages 49–51) for each player
- game markers, such as 1" construction paper squares
- copy of the reproducible teacher cards (pages 52 and 53), cut apart, shuffled, and placed in an envelope

Directions:

1. Give game markers and a gameboard to each child. Have her name each picture on her board. Provide assistance as necessary.

2. Explain that when she hears a letter that is the beginning letter of a picture on her board, she is to cover the picture with a marker.

3. Describe the criteria for winning: three in a row (vertically, horizontally, or diagonally) or four corners. Ask that winners say, "Sweet dreams!" to signal their wins.

4. To play, remove a card from the envelope and read the letter aloud. (Place it faceup for later reference.) Students who have a picture that begins with the named letter cover it. (A child may cover only one picture at a time.)

5. Play continues until someone calls out, "Sweet dreams!" To verify her win, have the child uncover and say the name of each picture and its beginning letter as you check her responses.

Sweet Dreams
Beginning-Letters Game

Sweet Dreams
Beginning-Letters Game

Sweet Dreams
Beginning-Letters Game

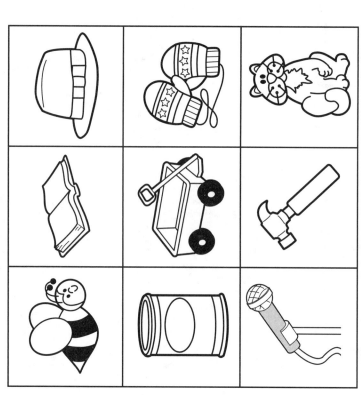

Sweet Dreams
Beginning-Letters Game

Sweet Dreams
Beginning-Letters Game

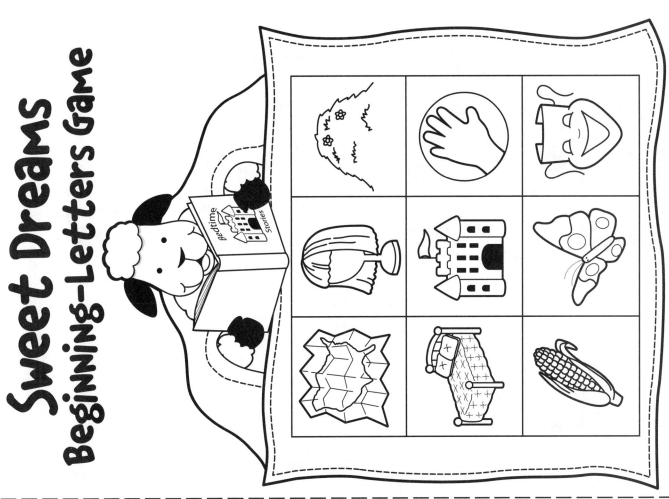

Sweet Dreams
Beginning-Letters Game

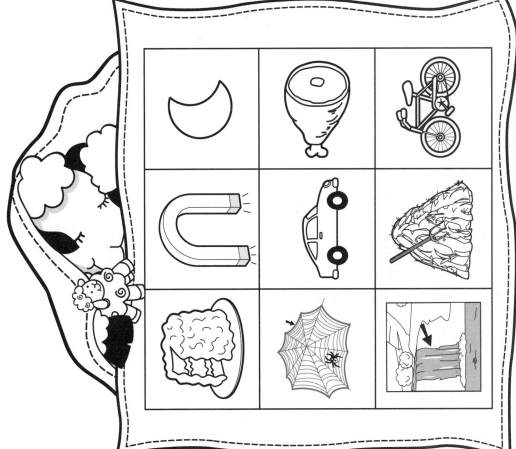

51

Reproducible Teacher Cards

Use with the directions on page 48.

B b   B b

TEC61061   TEC61061

C c   C c

TEC61061   TEC61061

H h   H h

TEC61061   TEC61061

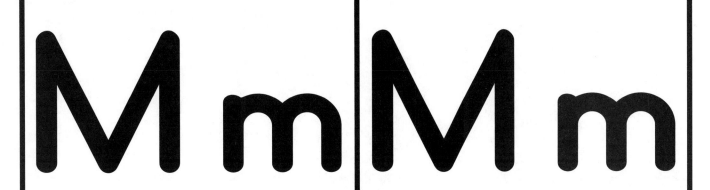

M m   M m

TEC61061   TEC61061

W w   W w

TEC61061   TEC61061

Ready to Paint
Beginning-Letters Game
d, f, g, l, p

What you need:

- gameboard copy (pages 55–57) for each player

- game markers, such as 1" construction paper squares

- copy of the reproducible teacher cards (pages 58 and 59), cut apart, shuffled, and placed in an envelope

Directions:

1. Give game markers and a gameboard to each child. Have him name each picture on his board. Provide assistance as necessary.

2. Explain that when he hears a letter that is the beginning letter of a picture on his board, he is to cover the picture with a marker.

3. Describe the criteria for winning: three in a row (vertically, horizontally, or diagonally) or four corners. Ask that winners say, "Wet paint!" to signal their wins.

4. To play, remove a card from the envelope and read the letter aloud. (Place it faceup for later reference.) Students who have a picture that begins with the named letter cover it. (A child may cover only one picture at a time.)

5. Play continues until someone calls out, "Wet paint!" To verify his win, have the student uncover and say the name of each picture and its beginning letter as you check his responses.

See page 75 for a student assessment page.

Ready to Paint
Beginning-Letters Game

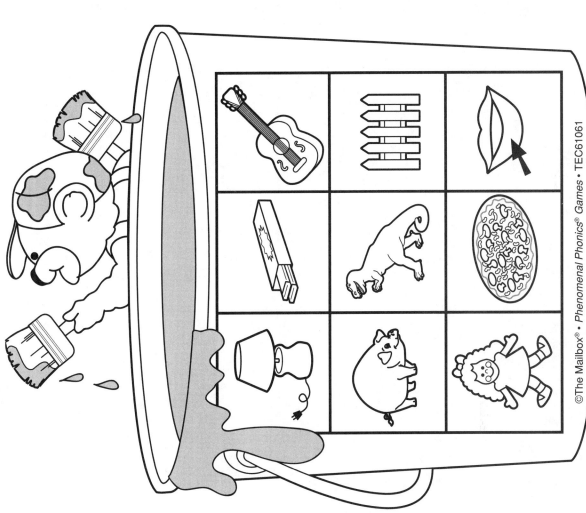

Ready to Paint
Beginning-Letters Game

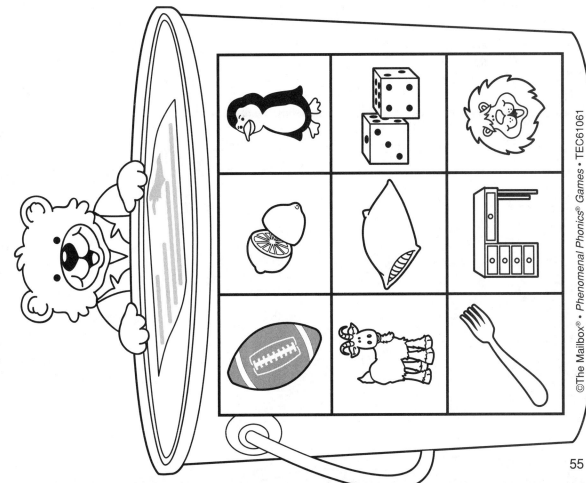

Ready to Paint
Beginning-Letters Game

Ready to Paint
Beginning-Letters Game

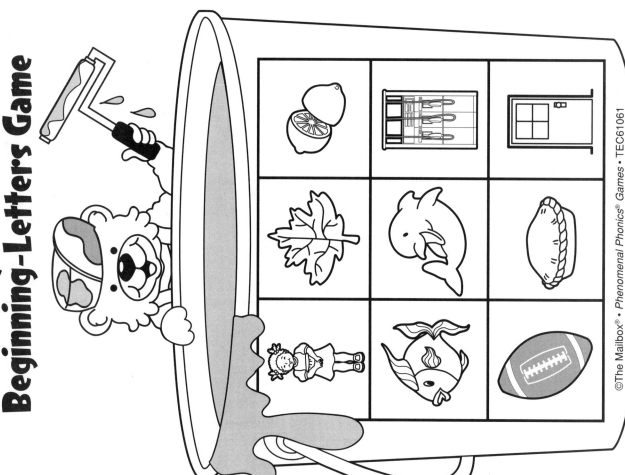

Ready to Paint
Beginning-Letters Game

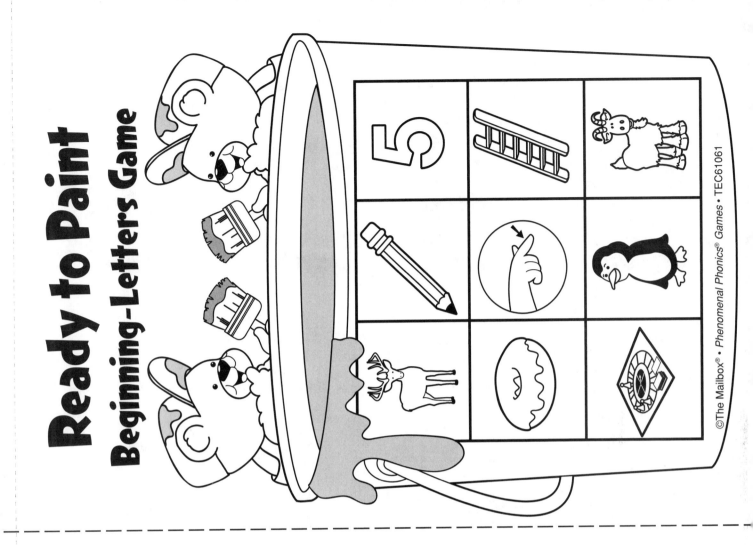

Ready to Paint
Beginning-Letters Game

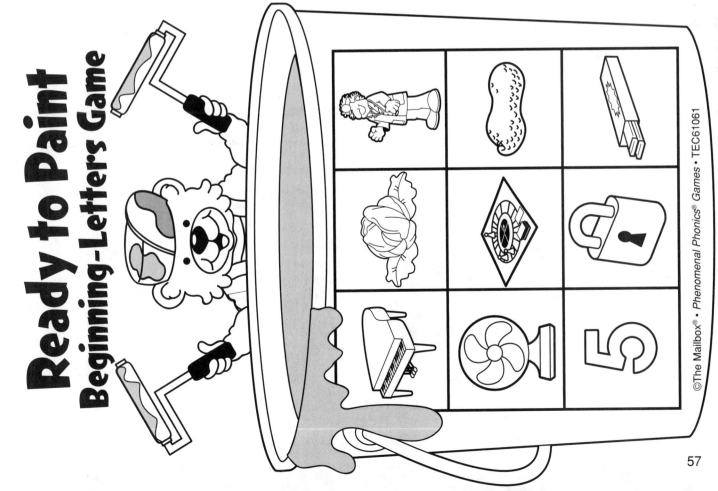

D d	D d
TEC61061	TEC61061
F f	F f
TEC61061	TEC61061
G g	G g
TEC61061	TEC61061

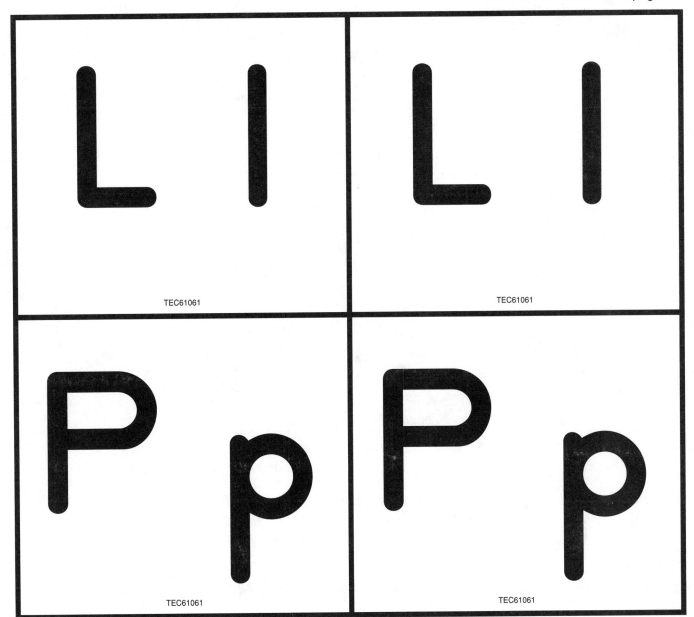

TEC61061

TEC61061

TEC61061

TEC61061

Diving Discoveries
Digraphs Game
ch, sh, th

- gameboard copy (pages 61–63) for each player
- game markers, such as 1" construction paper squares
- copy of the reproducible teacher cards (pages 64 and 65), cut apart, shuffled, and placed in an envelope

Directions:

1. Give game markers and a gameboard to each child. Review the three digraph sounds featured on each gameboard.

2. Explain that when the child hears a word, she listens for its beginning sound. If she has a matching digraph on her board, she is to cover it with a marker.

3. Describe the criteria for winning: four in a row (horizontally, vertically, or diagonally) or fill the board. Ask that winners say, "Splish, splash!" to signal their wins.

4. To play, remove a card from the envelope and say the name of the picture aloud. If desired, also show students the picture card. (Place it faceup for later reference.) Students who have a matching digraph cover it. (A child may cover only one digraph at a time.)

5. Play continues until someone calls out, "Splish, splash!" To verify her win, have the child uncover and say the sound of each digraph as you check her responses.

See page 77 for a student assessment page.

Diving Discoveries
Digraphs Game

ch ch	ch	th	ch
ch ch	ch ch	sh	th
sh	th	sh	th
sh sh sh	sh sh sh	sh	sh

Diving Discoveries
Digraphs Game

th th	th	sh	ch
th th	th	sh sh	sh
th	ch	sh	ch
ch ch ch	ch ch	sh ch ch	sh

Diving Discoveries
Digraphs Game

ch ch	ch	th	th
th	sh	sh	sh
th	ch	sh	sh
sh sh	sh	th	th sh

Diving Discoveries
Digraphs Game

sh sh	sh	ch	ch
th	ch	ch	sh
sh	ch	th	th
th	sh	th	th

Diving Discoveries
Digraphs Game

th	sh	ch	ch
th	th	th	ch
th	sh	sh	ch
sh sh	th sh	ch th	ch

Diving Discoveries
Digraphs Game

sh	th	th	ch
sh	ch	th	sh
sh	ch	ch	th
th	sh sh	ch ch	sh ch

Reproducible Teacher Cards

Use with the directions on page 60.

TEC61061

TEC61061

TEC61061

TEC61061

TEC61061

TEC61061

TEC61061

TEC61061

TEC61061

TEC61061

TEC61061

TEC61061

TEC61061

TEC61061

TEC61061

TEC61061

TEC61061

TEC61061

TEC61061

TEC61061

TEC61061

Name _____ Assessment of lowercase letters

Fluffy's Feast

Listen and do.

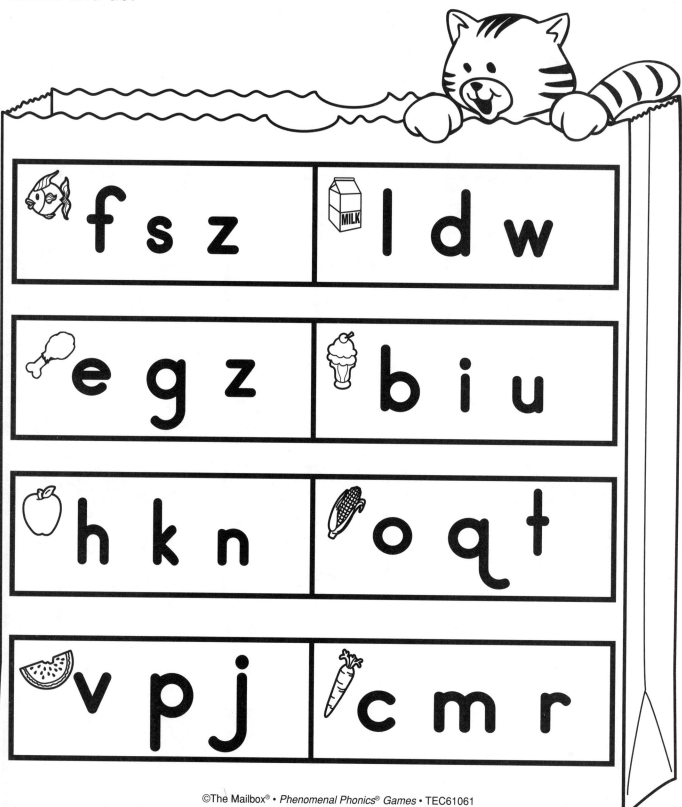

f s z   l d w

e g z   b i u

h k n   o q t

v p j   c m r

©The Mailbox® • Phenomenal Phonics® Games • TEC61061

Note to the teacher: Use with the directions on page 6. Prior to student use, make a master copy by circling one letter in each set. Give each student an unmarked copy and have him find the set with the fish picture. Then announce the circled letter on your copy and ask students to circle it on their papers. Continue in the same manner for each remaining set. Repeat as desired to assess other letters.

Up, Up, and Away!

Listen and do.

A	Q	M	
K	O	Z	
R	B	T	
G	W	E	
V	Y	J	
X	L	U	
F	N	I	
P	H	D	

Note to the teacher: Use with the directions on page 12. Prior to student use, make a master copy by circling one letter in each set. Give each student an unmarked copy and have her find the set by the elephant picture. Then announce the circled letter on your copy and ask students to circle it on their papers. Continue in the same manner for each remaining set. Repeat as desired to assess other letters.

Name _____

Out of This World

Listen and do.

☀	A	t	R	b	S	r
☾	G	N	l	g	U	x
☆	h	y	W	C	H	d
🛸	q	E	J	m	e	O
☁	F	p	K	Z	i	f

Note to the teacher: Use with the directions on page 18. Prior to student use, make a master copy by circling one letter (or two) in each row. Give each student an unmarked copy and have him find the row with the sun picture. Then announce the circled letter on your copy and ask students to circle it on their papers. Continue in the same manner for each remaining row. Repeat as desired to assess other letters.

School Tools

Circle the pictures in each row with matching beginning sounds.

Note to the teacher: Use with the directions on page 24.

Name _____

Bookworm's Notes

Circle the pictures in each row with matching beginning sounds.

		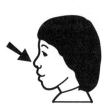		

Note to the teacher: Use with the directions on page 30.

Dragon Friends

Circle the pictures in each row
with matching beginning sounds.

A Sound Celebration

Circle the pictures in each set with matching beginning sounds.

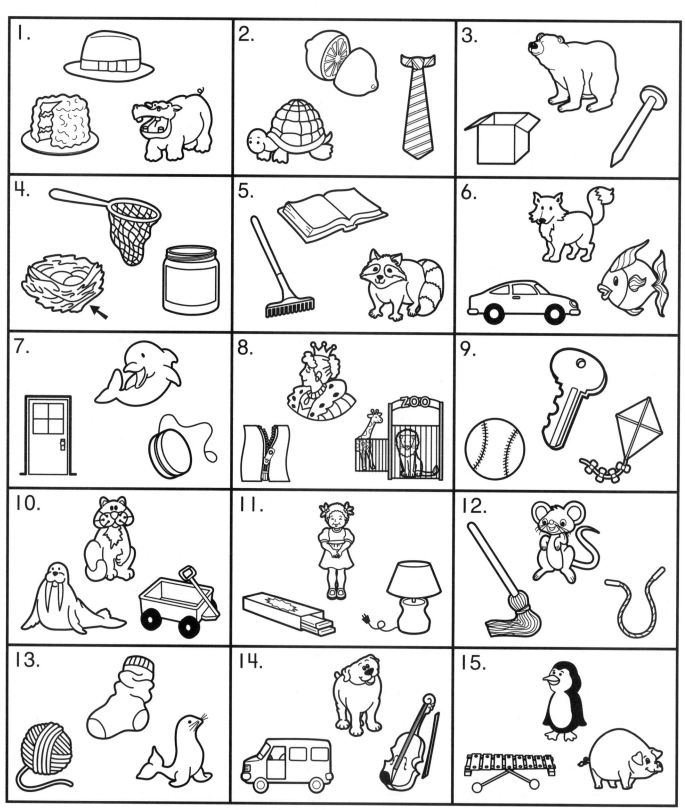

Look Who's Reading

Circle the pictures in each row with matching beginning letters.

n					
j					
s					
r					
t					

Note to the teacher: Use with the directions on page 42.

Sweet Dreams

Circle the pictures in each row with matching beginning letters.

Note to the teacher: Use with the directions on page 48.

Ready to Paint

Circle the pictures in each row
with matching beginning letters.

A Letter Celebration

Circle the picture in each set with the matching beginning letter.

Note to the teacher: Use after completing the games described on pages 42, 48, and 54.

Name _____

Diving Discoveries

Circle the pictures in each row with matching digraphs.

Note to the teacher: Use with the directions on page 60.

Storage Labels

Copy and cut out the storage labels on pages 78–80. Glue each label to a large manila envelope. Then place copies of the corresponding student gameboards and teacher cards inside each envelope. If desired, store game markers, a copy of the corresponding teacher page, and brag tags in each envelope as well.

Use with the games described on pages 6 and 12.

Out of This World
Uppercase- and Lowercase-Letters Game

TEC61061

School Tools
Beginning-Sounds Game
/f/, /m/, /r/, /s/, /t/

TEC61061

Bookworm's Notes
Beginning-Sounds Game
/d/, /k/, /n/, /p/, /w/

TEC61061

Dragon Friends
Beginning-Sounds Game
/b/, /g/, /h/, /v/, /z/

TEC61061

Storage Labels

Use with the games described on pages 42, 48, 54, and 60.

Look Who's Reading
Beginning-Letters Game
j, n, r, s, t

TEC61061

Sweet Dreams
Beginning-Letters Game
b, c, h, m, w

TEC61061

Ready to Paint
Beginning-Letters Game
d, f, g, l, p

TEC61061

Diving Discoveries
Digraphs Game
ch, sh, th

TEC61061